STUDIO SERIES™ BY PETER PAUPER PRES

KALEIDOSCOPE DESIGNS

ARTIST'S COLORING BOOK

Illustrated by Martha Day Zschock

PETER PAUPER PRESS, INC.
White Plains, NY

PETER PAUPER PRESS
Fine Books and Gifts Since 1928

OUR STORY

In 1928, at the age of twenty-two, Peter Beilenson began printing books on a small press in the basement of his parents' home in Larchmont, New York. Peter—and later, his wife, Edna—sought to create fine books that sold at "prices even a pauper could afford."

Today, still family owned and operated, Peter Pauper Press continues to honor our founders' legacy—and our customers' expectations—of beauty, quality, and value.

Illustrations © Martha Day Zschock
Designed by Heather Zschock

Copyright © 2015
Peter Pauper Press, Inc.
202 Mamaroneck Avenue
White Plains, NY 10601
All rights reserved
ISBN 978-1-4413-1839-8
Printed in China
7 6 5 4 3 2 1

www.peterpauper.com